WHY I HATE
MODERN ART

WHY I HATE MODERN ART

MODERN ART

Eli Levin

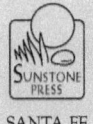

SUNSTONE
PRESS

SANTA FE

Sunstone books may be purchased for educational, business, or sales promotional use.
For information please write: Special Markets Department, Sunstone Press,
P.O. Box 2321, Santa Fe, New Mexico 87504-2321.

Body typeface › Bell MT
Printed on acid-free paper
∞

Library of Congress Cataloging-in-Publication Data

Levin, Eli, 1938-
Why I hate modern art / by Eli Levin.
    pages cm
Includes bibliographical references and index.
ISBN 978-0-86534-967-4 (softcover : alk. paper)
1. Modernism (Art) 2. Art movements. I. Title.
N6465.M63L48 2013
709.04--dc23

                    2013028527

WWW.SUNSTONEPRESS.COM
SUNSTONE PRESS / POST OFFICE BOX 2321 / SANTA FE, NM 87504-2321 /USA
(505) 988-4418 / ORDERS ONLY (800) 243-5644 / FAX (505) 988-1025

CONTENTS

Preface

The Education of a Realist Artist

My parents and stepparents were concerned with culture. They all encouraged me to express myself, and I painted a lot as a child.

When I was in junior high school, my father rented an apartment from an analyst who kept the front room for his office. In the entranceway, his waiting room, there were *Art News* magazines dating back about ten years. I poured over them.

After school, I went to the 96th Street Library and sat on the floor in front of the shelves of art books. Every page with a reproduction was hand-stamped with the library's logo, sometimes right on the image.

I went to Music and Art High School in New York City. This school provided an exceptionally broad grounding, a better art education than most I've experienced since.

I took drawing classes outside of school, evenings and weekends. Friday nights I went to Art Students League classes given by John Groth. We drew from the nude. Also, we always carried sketchbooks. Groth wanted us to do at least five drawings a day. I filled twenty of these hundred-page books. In addition, we brought to class compositional studies on assigned subjects, such as turmoil, harmony, a fight, love. From these studies and Groth's comments, we learned the basics of composition and illustration.

Most of Groth's students were adults. The only other teenage student was Robert Smithson, who later became a famous Earth Artist. He and I were the best of friends. In 1955, Bob and I organized a Saturday drawing group with some of my fellow Music and Art students. We took turns modeling (clothed). Fifty years later, I sold two drawings of Bob to the National Portrait Gallery.

Many of my high school friends were the children of left-wing Jewish intellectuals. Visiting their homes I saw paintings and graphics by the Soyer brothers, Philip Evergood, David Burlick, Jack Levine, Ben Shahn; etchings by Käthe Kollwitz; lithos by Daumier. There were also reproductions of Modigliani, Soutine, Pascin, Chagall, Rivera, Orozco, Benton, Curry, Wood and Marsh.

My high school girlfriend was Mimi Gross. Her father, the sculptor Chaim Gross, had a major art collection of American Moderns—Joseph Stella, Max Weber, Arshile Gorky, and more. Mimi later married Red Grooms.

Smithson and I used to go to the galleries every Saturday. About 20 of them were on 57th Street in little walk-up buildings. A.C.A. and Midtown were two of our favorites. A.C.A. exhibited Social Realists, mostly Communists. Midtown, run by Edith Halpert, had the best Americans of all styles from between the world wars.

Art museums were different when I was a student. They were private sanctuaries. They did not appeal to the public; there were no media hypes, blockbuster exhibitions, glitzy gift shops or trendy cafeterias.

The Whitney was on Eighth Street. The Guggenheim was in a brownstone on Fifth Avenue and had strictly non-objective art, as its original name, the Museum of Non-Objective Painting, indicated.

The Metropolitan Museum was peaceful, nearly empty. There was a big smoking room with plush couches and windows overlooking Central Park. Its walls were hung with Corots, and later with marvelous French academy paintings by Vibert: fat, funny bishops and cardinals.

During my high school years the Whitney moved to 54th Street and was connected to the Museum of Modern Art by an obscure passageway. I missed the Eighth Street space where the Whitney annuals had been reassuring, showing artists we were familiar with.

On 54th Street the annuals were full of painters we didn't know. Raphael Soyer was one of the few realists they kept showing.

The Museum of Modern Art had a number of rooms full of Realist art. These little rooms featured Depression art, European figurative art, Mexican art, Independent Realists, and Magic Realists. The most popular painting in the museum was Pavel Tchelitchew's *Hide and Seek*, a garish pseudo-surrealist image of a tree in which the spaces between the branches morphed into children.

The art schools I went to between 1956 and 1966 encouraged permissiveness. I sought out artists from the Depression era whose work I admired, but no one would teach anything except "express yourself." I drew under George Grosz one summer at Skowhegan. Then I studied painting from the nude with Raphael Soyer three hours a day, five days a week for two years. Neither Grosz nor Soyer had much to say. They were old and bitter because of the popularity of Abstract art.

Most of my teachers resented Abstract art, complaining that it was taking over everywhere.

Soyer put me in contact with a group of young artists who planned to picket the Museum of Modern Art. Soyer, along with Jack Levine, John Koch, and Edward Hopper, were backing the protest. But these four would not come to the meetings or lend their names publicly. I wrote the pamphlet that we distributed at the demonstration, a Marxist diatribe.

I looked for a place to show my work, without success. Soyer said he had to reserve the few connections he still had for his cronies, old artists fallen on hard times. He had a wall in his studio featuring his friends' work, but not his students'. I began to understand that we had been taught to paint in a passé style, anathema to the current art scene.

The few Realist galleries, having trouble selling their older artists, were not enthusiastic about a new generation of Social Realists. Several years out of art school, my work continued to be rejected.

When we turned eighteen in 1956, Smithson and I started hanging out at the Cedar Bar, mixing with the crowd, the hangers-on of the Abstract Expressionists.

On Friday and Saturday evenings, partygoers flocked through the dark loft neighborhoods. Parties were crowded, dark, very noisy. We didn't know the hosts, we didn't even know the guests. We brought our own bottle and got drunk and felt important.

Smithson was ambitious and eventually made connections in the Cedar Bar crowd. His art underwent many transformations, while mine remained Realist.

I went on to the Boston Museum School. The other students painted like Matisse on drugs, while I painted little figurative egg temperas. After a year and a half, I had half a year to go. Jan Cox, the head of the painting department, told me to paint more abstractly, twenty times larger and in oils if I wanted to graduate. I walked out.

When I was twenty-one, my father moved to Israel. He passed along to me his syndicated newspaper column, *Inside Art.* The column covered the New York art scene. For two years, I interviewed artists, covered exhibits, and reviewed art books. I wrote the first reviews of Red Grooms, Jim Dine, Claes Oldenburg, and, of course, Bob Smithson. Mostly I wrote about unknown Realists.

During the 1960s and 1970s, the art world was obsessed with being avant-garde.

By 1964, I despaired of the art scene and wandered westward, ending up in New Mexico. It was an art scene, but no one cared about New York; they were just artists.

Introduction

This book concerns my dedication to Realism in art and, concomitantly, why I hate Modern Art. Mine is a drastically revisionist history of Modern Art. The progression of "isms" is for me a regression. For me, twentieth century art is inferior in quality to Western art's preceding five centuries.

When I do have a good word for twentieth century art, it is usually reserved for Realists, especially those of the 1930s, as well as the few outsiders who went against the dominant trends. However, this book is not so much an appreciation of the resistance as it is a critique of the widely acclaimed development of Abstract art.

Why has abstraction so emphatically replaced representation? Why has avant-garde thinking denied the framework of perceptions and assumptions on which traditional art values were built? Why have art movements moved away from the common perceptions and sentiments that those few of us who still paint figurative art see and feel?

To me as an artist, the past still pertains. The experiences embodied in past art correspond to my experiences. My vision corresponds to that of earlier artists. For me, much of the purpose of art lies in its continuity, in the correspondences between art works. Earlier artists anticipated my concerns. Hopefully, future art lovers will share my perceptions.

Much of art is a witnessing. "I saw this," Goya often wrote under his etchings. Even if we don't grasp the complex history of Napoleon's invasion of Spain, Goya's reaction is with us, causing us to share his feelings.

Within the Western tradition, artists have recorded a tremendous range of related facts, ideas, and feelings. Modern artists avoid most of this accumulated history.

How significant can art be if it doesn't resonate with the continuity of culture?

A curious fact of Modern Art is that there has been almost no criticism against it. There has also been little intelligent discussion of Realism. Countless books, for over a century, have pursued the same line of argument, praising the virtues of avant-gardism.

My point of view is pretty much what Modern Art writers disdain.

The Evolution of This Book

For years I thought of writing a criticism of Modern Art. I was set off by an obscure book in my brother's library in Jerusalem: *A Treatise on Painting* by Harold Speed, written in 1924. Speed was a reactionary old fogey, an English portrait artist who deplored the cataclysm of twentieth century art:

> "At the present, when inner life is so disturbed and troubled, and so much concerned with material things that it is apt to be shallow, the artist is thrown back on his own individual feelings unsupported by any sustained weight of emotional life in the community . . . You therefore find artists frittering away their energies in experimenting with new and amusing manners of expression . . . There is too much striving for aggressive and self-centered individuality and not enough of the artist losing himself in the deeper current of the emotional life of his time."

Speed observed that even minor painters from previous centuries were able to project a sureness about existence, a sense of being immersed in life. This he saw as missing from all Modern Art.

Where Did Art Go Bad?

My analysis follows the development of Modern Art chronologically. Starting somewhat ironically with the self-proclaimed "first Realist," Gustave Courbet, I continue down the rushing torrent of "isms" to the stagnancy of the Post-Modern.

The cascade of isms tore away at the canons of art that were still upheld throughout most of the nineteenth century, the knowledge of the great academies that extended through the high Renaissance, Baroque, Neoclassical and Romantic periods. From 1850 to 1900, over three generations, the skills needed for complex representation were lost. Not only did the skills disappear, but also their underlying premises: the humanistic and traditional comprehension of life. The accumulated knowledge of art practice was thrown onto the "garbage heap of history."

The seeds of the dissolution were already in the Romantics' endorsement of rebellion, in their conceiving of an avant-garde. After that, each successive movement rejected the chief qualities of its predecessor. Each new concept was more exclusive, more vehemently reductive, ultimately a *reductio ad absurdum.*

The Academies

One of the events art history fails to adequately explain is the loss of the traditional art academies. The French salons, which exhibited academic art and have been vilified in retrospect, were society's greatest manifestation of art for the people. More people saw more art and liked it better than at any other time in history. We pay lip service to democracy and freedom, but for over a hundred years our art historians have been vilifying the art of the salons, never daring to suggest that any academic art was as good as any work of the Impressionists.

The academics were maintaining the standards of the Western tradition, while successive rebels discarded every quality of past art. An invasion of barbarians would not have been more destructive than the late nineteenth century avant-garde.

Ingres' dictum, written over his studio door, "Drawing is the probity of art," is dead language to us, doubly so as people have forgotten what "probity" means. Perspective and the third dimension have been thrown out Leonardo's window. Techniques such as underpainting and glazing are forgotten. The Classical and Christian cultures with their iconography are no longer accessible. The major themes of life: ages of man, family, heroism, sacrifice, tragedy, love—none of these are considered depictable subjects. Beauty itself is considered passé, especially in the human form.

The public goes to movies and sees any or all of these themes. They might even be cajoled into watching a Greek tragedy. But if shown a painting by Jean Leon Gerome or Paul Delaroche that deals with the same theme, and even uses the same effects (which clever film directors have appropriated), the public is advised to sneer.

I used to think that if museums would only show academic art, the public would like it better than Impressionism. Or that even twentieth century Realism would be more popular than Abstract art.

I'm no longer sure. Even if there were not incessant proselytizing in favor of Modern Art, the public, used to the quick fix, would probably find academic art too subtle and erudite. The aesthetic, historical, and literary references would be beyond their grasp. As far back as the 1870s it became apparent that the nouveau riche were uncomfortable with history painting. For them, a sunny park had more resonance than Shakespeare.

If the Metropolitan Museum had a room with two paintings from their collection on opposite walls: Jackson Pollock's *Blue Poles* and Jacques Louis David's *Death of Socrates*, which would engage the public more? The desperate confusion of Pollock or the controlled clarity of David? Pollock's car crash certainly resonates more than Socrates' hemlock. Even if our modern viewer had read the *Phaedo*, would he understand better a wise man calmly accepting poison or a desperate man poisoning himself with alcohol?

The Met has a few academic paintings mixed with other outré nineteenth century styles in dimly lit rooms. The Impressionists are dazzlingly displayed in the brilliant central salon. What if academic art had an equal venue, with earphones, wall texts, lecturers, critical acclaim, books, college courses, auction records? Would the public prefer the daubs of Monet to the obsessive details of Meissonier? Would the male gaze be more attracted to the silken skinned lovelies of Bougereau or the garishly painted fleshpots of Renoir?

Courbet

In the history of the developing mediocrity of Modern Art, Gustave Courbet has the honor of being the first artist. In proclaiming that his work was Realistic he achieved the opposite, a self-consciousness that distanced him from the subjects he painted. Take for example his oxymoronic title *The Artist's Studio: an Allegory of the Real*. Whereas in previous art the "real" was taken for granted, Courbet made it a style. The real was conceived rather than embodied.

Courbet is a clumsy and unobservant painter. Rather than empathizing with reality he succeeds chiefly in projecting his own aggressive persona. By clumsy, I mean heavy-handed, awkward in the articulation of his figures, in proportions, in delineating space.

Courbet's "Realism" as a concept is the beginning of critical emphasis in art. Here "Realism" means contemporaneity, which implies the progress and progression of the new.

Baudelaire makes an appearance in *The Artist's Studio*. A host of literary men began proselytizing for the new in art, promoting each advance while claiming it was being held back by the bourgeoisie. These daring "rebels" were actually high-bourgeoisie tastemakers, setting themselves up as the prophets of cultural fashion. They condescended to and ultimately controlled popular taste. Their "anti-academic" academy has continued and prevailed for over 150 years, until today the cultural elite can perpetrate any absurdity and the public has no recourse but to accept it.

This trend reaches its apogee in Richard Serra's *Tilted Arc*. This oppressive steel wall was set up in a public plaza, which it rendered unusable. People who had enjoyed the area filed complaints and petitions. It took four years to get a hearing. Not one artist, art critic, art historian, or any other person in the art world could be found to speak against the piece. A jury finally voted to remove the sculpture.

Manet

Many Modernist historians say that Modern Art started with Edouard Manet. Roger Fry, for instance, brought an exhibition of Modernist French Art to London before the First World War. He called it *Manet and the Post-Impressionists*, skipping the Impressionists and thinking, I suppose, that they weren't modern enough.

Manet painted an early masterpiece, *Olympia*, a confrontational nude that was a milestone in the changing perception of women. Besides this revelation, the critics of his day also noticed that the lighting in the painting is dead on, minimizing shading and shadows. This made everything look flat, one of the shibboleths of twentieth century art.

Manet's other paintings also have a surprising flatness, spatial ambiguity, and lapses in scale. Before and especially after the concentrated effort of *Olympia*, his works are patchy, disengaged, and lack focused meaning. All this makes them modern. What were perceived as faults in Manet's day are now considered to be exciting innovations. A good example is his last major painting from 1882, *The Bar at the Folies-Bergeres*. While this is a lovely painting, there are weird incongruities in the reflections seen in the large mirror behind the major figure, the barmaid. These ambiguities are what modern critics focus on.

The Impressionists

While Courbet's self-conscious Realism was dark and airless, the Impressionists went too far in the opposite direction, letting light and color dominate what was depicted.

Doesn't bad drawing bother anyone? Deformed hands, necks disconnected from backbones, cutout bodies in shapeless clothes: must we accept all this in the name of bright color? We are told that these are impressions, entailing unresolved details. But how often the unresolved sloughs over into ignorance. Some examples: the figures in Monet's garden scenes; Pissarro's peasants; Cézanne's bathers.

Art writers praise the Impressionists' and Post-Impressionists' freedom from restraint, their self-expression. The more audacious the better. We are taught to admire the artist's will, his insouciance; we accept his every whim. We hardly dare question these creative geniuses. So what if the art no longer shows us hands we could imagine holding, clothes that could be worn, bodies that could be touched.

How quickly drawing was disregarded in the 1860s and 1870s. Manet's and Pissarro's hundreds of etchings are so lacking in draftsmanship that even by our standards they are embarrassing to contemplate and have been relegated to obscurity.

In praise of the Impressionists, there is great vitality in their having gone out into the landscape and done so much raw work. Their love of nature is contagious. It should be noted, however, that it was the previous generation who discovered nature. The Barbizon painters, the Italian Macchiaioli, even the English watercolorists, discovered painting outdoors. Art historians sometimes refer to these forerunners as "pre-Impressionists."

Monet

Monet has sureness of touch, which expresses a oneness with nature so pervasive that it becomes almost mechanical. There's a subtle shift away from the human warmth of the other Impressionists.

Monet's paintings, especially in the early and late periods, have a flat effect, endearing him to Modernists. In the late work, the paint surface is something like oatmeal and cement, often obscuring the texture of what is depicted.

Monet's biography, usually glossed over, is a chronicle of opportunism, ingratitude, and monomania. While his wife, Camille, was dying as a result of trying to abort his child, Monet was seducing his patron's wife. Monet was the only Impressionist missing from Degas' collection. Degas made the comment, "Would you dine with a man like that?"

Do these upsetting biographical facts make Monet any less of an artist? Personally, I find it harder to look at his work because of my negative feelings about him.

Pissarro and Sisley

The lyric poets of landscape were Pissarro and Sisley.

Pissarro had an endearing warmth, but he was clumsy. He depicted peasant figures in keeping with his radical socialist beliefs, but the figures were awkward even beyond their peasant status and often were spatially ambiguous in the landscapes.

Sisley, especially in his middle period, had perhaps the perfect Impressionist touch. At his best, his work evokes pure, idle pleasure. But unlike Monet's, Sisley's paintings often lack energy. He seems to be irresolute, his concentration wavering.

Renoir

Renoir should have been an academic artist. Like academics at their worst, he pandered to bad taste, painting cute children and simpering ingénues in pastel colors. He certainly had the prurient interest in female flesh of Cabanel or Bougereau. Renoir could draw general forms well, but in his later work they thicken and become globby.

Renoir's attempts at Modernity are not integral. He does not capture light, or the flicker of nature, and his scenes of contemporary life seem posed. His painting technique can be turgid, his rainbow palette strident. Renoir's compositional devices are limited. He often plumps his subject down in the middle of the canvas, fading the picture out at the edges.

Degas

Degas is the most complex artist of the Independents. He didn't consider himself an Impressionist, but rather a Realist. And his work does belong to the last phase of the Realist movement, the socially conscious depiction of contemporary life in a naturalistic style. Although this movement does not have a label and is not well documented, it is among other things the last manifestation of academic discipline.

It would be clear that Degas belongs to the academic camp if it weren't for his quirk of leaving so much unfinished. In Degas the parts are hardly ever homogenous. Besides unfinished areas, there are disparate kinds of focus, signifying contradictory intentions within one framework. This breakdown of academic vision is pleasing to most Modern viewers but for me, these focus problems are blips of interference, weakening Degas' otherwise incisive statements. To my mind, Degas' strongest paintings are the late pastels of women washing themselves.

The Independent Exhibitions

The eight exhibits in which the Impressionists took part between 1872 and 1884 were titled "The Independents" or "The Anonymous Society". Many of Degas' colleagues among the naturalists and Realists were included. With all the thousands of books on Impressionism, not one book has featured the non-Impressionist contingent of the Independent exhibitions. Art history extols the painters of refractory light effects, while maintaining silence concerning the painters who were more socially conscious. The fifth Independents exhibition in 1880 featured 18 artists. Non-Impressionist painters in the Independents included Zandomeneghi, Raffaelli, Caillebotte, Lebourg, Goeneutte, Cassatt, Bracquemond.

Post-Impressionism

Modernism endorses disengaged artists, seeing in them the social dysfunction of art. The very next generation after the Impressionists, unimaginatively called Post-Impressionists, were social misfits with a vengeance. Those three sainted, unhappy men, Van Gogh, Gauguin and Cézanne, are the patron saints of Modern aesthetic alienation.

These three giants of Post-Impressionism destroyed whatever remained of the traditional values of Western art.

The Impressionists still painted their subjects in a style that we consider beautiful. They avoided the traditional canons of beauty, but they substituted a fresh interpretation of nature's charms.

It is a remarkable fact that Van Gogh, Gauguin and Cézanne all studied with Pissarro. Camille Pissarro's humble deference to nature must have caused an overreaction in these antisocial egoists. They were mad to be themselves.

The three precursors of Modernism were obsessed with reinventing art, rejecting tradition, embracing autodidactic experiment, and finally, developing new styles. Reinventing art, each of the three gained obsessive command of a partial aesthetic. Ensuing generations of artists, inspired by the extremes of the Post-Impressionists, have continued the process of fragmentation.

If only the three Post-Impressionists could have been combined into one artist! This super-artist would have had Van Gogh's incisive drawing, deep space, and passion for humanity; Gauguin's poetry of pattern and color, and sense of mystery; Cézanne's dedication, obsession with structure, and painterly touch.

Vincent Van Gogh

Van Gogh's oeuvre is a cry for attention. There is no subtlety. His brush strokes are so insistent that they obscure what he is painting. We see the artist's turmoil more than the subject. Vincent Van Gogh's career from his first clumsy drawings to his last wild swirls spanned just ten years. (Students at the academy spent almost that much time learning draftsmanship even before they started to paint.)

Vincent is beloved by art students because he was the supreme student. They empathize with him, the very response that he was denied during his lifetime when standards were higher. Modern viewers are overwhelmed by sympathy, responding to the effort more than the achievement.

In Van Gogh's early work his intention was to make common cause with simple people. This was his essential motivation, but he lost sight of it in Paris. His feeling for people was deflected by an increased obsession with perception. Finally, even perception gives way to the act of painting. Most Modern students follow this progression.

When Van Gogh thought he could communicate humanistically, as in *The Potato Eaters*, his sincerity mitigated his touching clumsiness. Later he developed graphic incision and some painterly qualities, but also a loss of empathy and an increased sense of alienation.

Paul Gauguin

Gauguin is in many ways the father of Expressionism, though his style is softer and less dynamic. He was an odd combination of visionary and synthesizer: his movement was sometimes called syntheticism. He had the courage to formulate a style that combined organic shapes, primitive patterns, and personal poetic insights.

Having started late, Gauguin never learned to paint in the full sense, but rather filled in patterns. Gauguin showed the way for the use of decorative elements in Modern Art, even though his own tendency toward pattern and abstraction was subordinated to an internal symbolic vision.

The paintings of Tahitian women demonstrate a longing to reconfigure a standard of beauty. They are simultaneously denials of and variations on the classical nude tradition.

Although Gauguin was in search of new spiritual mystery, his work hangs onto the tradition of figure painting in the poses of Tahitian women. Hesitation and a desire to synthesize keep his paintings from being stridently modern. In this, Gauguin the artist was natural, feeling his way, combining observations and insights, fusing doubt with awe.

Paul Cézanne

It is my opinion that Cézanne could not draw. While he was obsessed with structure in some complicated way, he could not construct a solid figure, hardly even an apple. He juggled structural elements, but did not resolve the whole. The chief aspect of spatial perception that eluded Cézanne was linear continuity. He was blind to foreshortening and recession.

There are innumerable fancy theories about Cézanne's aesthetic, none of which are corroborated in his own writings, which are muddled. Cézanne wrote of the cylinder, the sphere and the cone, but didn't mention the cube. To my mind, he was incapable of accurate perception. His shortcomings evolved into stylistic quirks. Our century, enamored of the irrational, turned his quirks into dogmas.

Cézanne's drawings are in a class with the etchings of Manet and Pissarro. They comprise scribbly, fussy, nudgy, inconclusive forays at form. If he approximates one side, he loses the other. If he gets both sides, he squishes or bloats the middle. Inevitably, the adjacent part doesn't fit. In the academies they emphasized articulation of the joints: No such thing exists in Cézanne's work. When occasionally the parts are more or less in order, there's no sense of scale.

When Cézanne describes the back of a table, he starts the line on one level and it comes out on another. There's something pathetic in this. He's depicting luscious fruits, he's got myriad visceral little touches of rich paint (the "touches" that he claimed art was all about), it's all freshly observed, and then it falls short due to an apparent dyslexic lapse.

In Cézanne's paintings all the elements battle to be up front, there's no receding space. There's also no negative space, around or between forms, assuming they have edges. (Lack of negative space is considered a positive attribute, and is one of the commandments of Modernism, the gospel according to Clement Greenberg.) In Cézanne's paintings the effect is claustrophobic. The viewer is stymied trying to disengage the forms from their surroundings. True, this is part of the evidence of Cézanne's intense struggling. Modern viewers empathize, as they do with so much that is inept.

Van Gogh, Gauguin, and Cézanne wanted to have encompassing visions. They were Idealistic outsiders, full of quirky sincerity and dedication. Their ordeals recall Jacob wrestling with the angel, the subject of one of Gauguin's paintings.

The Nabis

Vuillard and Bonnard are the last two artists in the transition to Modernism who retained a feeling for nature and regard for humanity. They are afterthoughts of Impressionism, clarifying some small points while turning the intensity of Impressionism's discoveries into decoration.

Vuillard and Bonnard were conservative. Their backward-looking position achieved in charm what it lacked in conviction. Their paintings are tinged with enervation, glibness, satiety, but they are reassuring and imbued with warmth.

I prefer Vuillard to Bonnard because his draftsmanship is tighter. Bonnard's abound in flabby shapes and scribbly details. Vuillard's paint surface is tactile and sensual, while Bonnard's can look like smears and crusts of old food. Vuillard plays with deep space and contrasts of scale. Bonnard, like Cézanne, pushes everything up to the paint surface.

The fascination of Vuillard and Bonnard is in their intimate vision. In fact, their work is sometimes referred to as intimism. They draw us into their delectable private world. They are clearly influenced by Gauguin, with his internalized vision, warm colors, and the soft, decorative depiction of his surroundings. Vuillard and Bonnard carry the sense of intimacy further, with a Proustian claustrophobic immediacy of colors and shapes. Similar characteristics were also found in certain academic artists of the previous generation, such as Alfred Stevens and Tissot.

Unlike those two earlier painters of interiors, in Vuillard and Bonnard the appearance of effort is unthinkable. Theirs is a blasé insouciance. We want to be there, but we realize that this is their private domain, they are the insiders.

Vuillard and Bonnard are the last artists whose paintings reveal their comfort in their surroundings. Matisse wished to be seen that way, but he is constructing and projecting an image. There was already a hint of the mirage in Vuillard and Bonnard. Although they bodied forth the overwhelming detail of their daily lives, one wonders whether their paintings express personality or persona. Looking at a Renoir, we sense who he is. Vuillard and Bonnard are latter-day chroniclers of a Parisian feminine milieu similar to Renoir's, but their world verges on insubstantiality. From Vuillard and Bonnard it is a small step to the make-believe world of Matisse or Leon Bakst's designs for the Ballet Russe.

The Fauves

The Fauves took up where the Post-Impressionists left off, making a superficial mix of their disparate elements. The Fauves reveled in the new language of painting, a truncated vocabulary writ large. The Fauve style is still used to this day by young, overenthusiastic artists as an easy, exciting way to make art.

An especially liberating factor was the irrational use of color. To me, there is nothing more exasperating than the profusion of random garish colors that has been the hallmark of Modernism. Fauvism gave art a license that approaches arbitrariness.

The interaction of the Fauves couldn't last long. The imperative of avant-gardist change and the egoism of the participating artists demanded that they move on, do something different and individualistic.

The Progeny of the Three Fathers of Modern Art

Since the start of Modern Art we have had a century of confusing and contradictory aesthetic claims. There have been many revisions before art experts codified a selective progression of isms. Finally, it was decided that the high road of Modern Art commences with Cézanne, then continues through Cubism, Constructivism, Abstract Expressionism, and Minimalism.

Van Gogh had his descendants: some Fauves, Edvard Munch and the Expressionists, and sundry passionate souls since, such as Chaim Soutine, Jean Dubuffet, and Charles Burchfield. From Van Gogh there is also the narrative aspect for lovers of the downtrodden, which was well traveled during the Depression years. But now this is all considered a bit embarrassing, the awkward teenage years and heart on the sleeve of Modern Art.

Gauguin's progeny were more elegant but less intense than Van Gogh's: the Nabis, Henri Matisse, Mark Rothko, and all the decorative art that is perhaps too complacent to represent the tortured twentieth century.

It is the heritage of Cézanne, the deconstructed, the systemized and abstracted, even the dichotomous, clumsy, confused and contradictory, that has become emblematic of that century's self-image.

Cubism

Early Cubism is startlingly reductive: there is little there, and it's redundant. How abruptly so much has gone by the way. "Aha," we say to ourselves (or it is said to us), "all the rest was superfluous."

Art would soon be further reduced, but at the onset Cubism looked as if it had bared the structure of art. This was especially true of the early monochromatic brown Cubism that seemed to have the resonance of the old-fashioned varnished paintings but almost without space or subject matter.

The Cubists found it was no simple matter to re-flesh the skeleton. The substructure did not readily support a new superstructure. The second phase, synthetic Cubism, is appropriately named. The color, collage, figuration, symbolic and biomorphic forms were all frills that chafed against the structural limitations. Even Picasso, the magician with his brilliant draftsmanship and Expressionist machismo, was constrained by the stultifying faceting.

Guernica

Guernica, despite its many apologists, is to my mind the biggest failure of Cubism. The painting was a commission from the French government for the World's Fair, meant to demonstrate anti-fascist solidarity with the Spanish republic. Picasso depicted the victims of the fascist massacre using the stereotypes of classical battle iconography. He caricatured them in a cartoon style. He parodied dramatic shading by filling in his dark areas with a line pattern that suggests newspaper print. Scramble all this into the near illegibility of Cubist disjunction, and we have a caricature of art about war atrocity. *Guernica* expresses ironic remove and disaffection as strongly as it expresses empathy.

The art historians see in this picture an amazing wedding of the avant-garde and humanism. The aesthetic distancing is construed as making Social Realism palpable.

There is a series of drawings relating to *Guernica*. They were made after the painting, the reverse of traditional practice. Were they compensatory? They are more expressive than the painting, but do they deplore violence, or celebrate it?

Picasso's Fame

Artists of the twentieth century have worked in the shadow of Picasso's overbearing image.

When Picasso scribbled on a napkin, some sycophant crawled under the table to retrieve the masterpiece. One of his ex-lovers kept his fingernail clippings in a jar. There are more books about Picasso than any other artist in history. Picasso combines nineteenth-century creativity with twentieth-century media glut.

The quality of his individual works is not as significant as the enormous conglomerate or the accumulated aggression behind the works.

Picasso and Tradition

The classical tradition understood art as the ideal, the beautiful, the perfect, the purified. Even negative emotions were clarified, seen in a larger context. With characteristic bravura, Picasso was always demonstrating that he could draw as well as the Masters. He did not have their intentions, however. Picasso's purpose was to show off, to get attention, to dominate. There was no resolution in his oeuvre—Picasso obsessively repeated himself. The elements of his style became brutalized, self-referential.

By resolution, I mean when a period of an artist's work is summed up in an encompassing work. The two "masterpieces," *Mademoiselles d'Avignon* and *Guernica*, while grand, are more breakthroughs than summations. It seems clear that Picasso had a short attention span.

Matisse

Despite what I have said, Picasso was a Master compared to Matisse. Though Matisse was a superficial draftsman, he made a virtue of his shortcomings, and is celebrated for his free-flowing lines. For "free" read "flaccid."

With Matisse, proportions were subjected to arbitrary changes. There is a series of reproductions of a painting of a nude that he changed a hundred times. Why? If there was a reason why Matisse changed shapes, it was so that they would lose their particular meanings and become decoration.

This same arbitrariness liberated color and flattened space. Matisse's indifference to spatial structure precluded his partaking in the rigors of Cubism. Spatial denial made Matisse the prototype for Modernism's ideological insistence on the inviolability of the picture plane.

In a famous statement, Matisse insisted on an easy art, composed of simple shapes and pleasant colors. There were no interesting subjects or ideas. One might have thought that a woman's body could exert some fascination, until one sees how Matisse reduced bodies to generic ciphers of complacency, less stimulating than the patterns and colors around them. Matisse achieved his goal, that art should be like "sinking into an easy chair."

Vuillard and Bonnard were more old-fashioned than Matisse. Their painterly touches make us feel the superfluity of our world of plastic, while Matisse's detached images are harbingers of the plastic look. Unlike Vuillard and Bonnard, Matisse's works gain in reproduction.

Non-Objective Artists

In early non-objective art there is usually a lack of interest in spatial structure. This can be contrasted to Cubism, which still had a sensual response to shallow space. With the non-objective artists, we enter the realm of graphic design. Design was revitalized by the Russian avant-garde, but oddly, the two artists credited with being the first did not adapt that well to graphic design. Kasimir Malevich was heavy-handed. One has only to compare his paintings to the other Russian Constructivist, Wassily Kandinsky, who, especially in the early works, was chaotic.

The Three Ks

Paul Klee's oeuvre tends toward problem solving at one extreme and cartooning at the other.

Frantisek Kupka had a period of lush romantic abstraction, enhanced by mysticism.

In Wassily Kandinsky's early fantasy paintings, the palette is over-rich. His first non-objective works manage to break away from the candy coating, and they generate considerable excitement. Their chaotic frenzy gave way to increasing order, with a concomitant loss of painterliness. As Kandinsky's style evolved there was a loss of touch, a systematizing. However, the floating geometric shapes did add order and scale.

The rules for abstraction were codified, largely due to Kandinsky's writings, and non-objective art became easy. For the next thirty years, bland abstractions were produced all over the world. They still are.

The culminating decadent phase of non-objective art was Abstract Expressionism. It was an American mixture of ego-driven action painting and bloated non-objective art.

American Modernism

All the major ideas of Modern Art were already expressed by 1920. The whole momentum from Post-Impressionism to Dada lasted thirty years, one long generation. In art history texts it is stretched out as a succession of movements, mini-generations, lasting only about five years each. Some irresolute artists switched every few years trying to keep up.

In the 1920s artists were spinning their wheels, even backtracking. They found it was awkward to retreat, as this violated the raison d'être of the avant-garde. After the Great War there was a longing for "Return to Order." Many artists hesitated to abandon their signature styles for the vagaries of endless experiment. They dug in, each cultivating his own personality cult. During this process of institutionalizing their own styles, many artists retreated from universal abstraction and even adopted nationalist themes. Examples: Picasso's classical period, De Chirico's Roman period, Matisse's odalisques, Leger's workers, Steiglitz's Early American Moderns painting Maine, New Mexico, Pennsylvania in his new gallery called "An American Place."

1920s and 1930s Realism

In the 1920s and particularly in the 1930s there was a renewed interest in Realism. This was particularly strong in artists of the left, who wanted to emphasize socialist and humanist themes. Ironically, the Nazis and Russian Communists also favored traditional Idealist and Realist art, with subtle and sometimes disturbing differences.

Exceptions to the avant-garde theory are usually ignored in art histories. Clement Greenberg's much-referenced early essay, *Avant-Garde and Kitsch*, equates American Realism with totalitarian thinking. After that he ignores any kind of storytelling art.

I have always liked Social Realist and regional art. I love the human scale, the social concern. Despite the loss of traditional European art techniques, despite the scorn of elitist art theorists like Alfred Barr at the Museum of Modern Art, the Depression-era artists depicted the world around them with conviction.

The art of the 1920s and 1930s, worldwide, is not given its due. Mexico had Diego Rivera and Jose Clemente Orozco; the United States had Thomas Hart Benton and Edward Hopper. In Germany there were George Grosz and Otto Dix; in England Stanley Spencer and in France Boucheron; in Italy Giorgio Morandi and Renato Guttuso. There are many more.

Stieglitz Stable

Unlike the Modernist European painters who influenced them, the Stieglitz group had little interest in the figure, probably because of lack of training. The Cubists and school of Paris artists still emphasized the human element, however fragmented.

The Americans saw streamlined shapes, symbols, and signs. They painted bluntly, lacking the European "touch." The Americans had no lingering fascination with the development of the image, none of the Europeans' concern with delineating, articulating, and refining. Works by the Stieglitz group tend to be bold, simplistic, unfortunately influenced by folk art.

Despite their faux naïf traits, the Stieglitz artists were self-consciously avant-garde, above the prosaic American lifestyle. They were proud of being different, precious, even effete.

John Marin

John Marin was the most promoted and overrated Stieglitz artist. His style is manic, everything twitching around, pushing forward. Marin developed a predictable shorthand: a triangle is a sailboat, a wiggly line is water. This becomes tiresome.

One of Marin's claims to fame is that he freed up watercolor techniques. Is this a blessing? Marin's slash and splash strokes, spotted on the blank paper, are spontaneous enough, but he blinded generations of artists to watercolor's potential subtlety.

Marsden Hartley

Marsden Hartley, like Charles Demuth, never quite found his style. Their approaches were opposite: Demuth insinuated; Hartley was bombastic.

Hartley made forays into Blue Rider, Die Brucke, Cubism, biomorphism, precisionism, regionalism, and primitivism. Hartley also wrote purple prose, poems, and aesthetic theory. He described O'Keeffe as the quintessential female artist, equating her flower paintings to women's genitalia, a critique that was deeply offensive to her.

Georgia O'Keeffe

Georgia O'Keeffe was the strongest of the Stieglitz stable. Her paintings of flowers have monolithic presence. I find something very removed about her work that leaves me with an empty feeling. Her style is a closed system, a subtle dissociation from perception. Still, her paintings do express her considerable self-contained will power.

Arthur Dove

Arthur Dove's work is similar to O'Keeffe's, but has more directness and intimacy. Dove versus O'Keeffe, Demuth versus Hartley, Braque versus Picasso: sensibility as opposed to power.

Dove was the most consistently Abstract of the Stieglitz entourage, the only one whose work stayed Abstract during the 1920s and 1930s. He was one of the earliest non-objective artists. There is very little development in his output; his visual vocabulary is simple, sometimes bland. Ironically, of the Stieglitz group, Dove's work is the most imbued with the sensation of nature.

Alfred Stieglitz

Stieglitz championed easy forms of abstraction: clear, understandable, even amusing: he seemed to be propounding that anyone can do Modern Art if they only dare. He was America's guru of Modernism. Artists returning from Europe, disoriented, contended for his attention. Those not admitted into his circle seemed unable to maintain their complex European insights in an America that lacked contexts. Stieglitz was adroit in building a bridge from European to American taste. At his first gallery, "291," his artists reveled in new international aesthetics, contrasting them to the backward provinciality of home culture. But after the First World War, Stieglitz consolidated his position and opened a new gallery, "An American Place." The European innovations were willfully adapted to the home market. Stieglitz emphasized, chauvinistically, that John Marin painted Maine; O'Keeffe, New Mexico; and Hartley both. Demuth painted New Jersey. Their visual colloquialisms were extolled by the poet, William Carlos Williams, a close friend of Stieglitz. Only Arthur Dove remained impervious to this Americana, perhaps because he lived on a houseboat.

Two Muralists

Thomas Hart Benton and Diego Rivera, even more than the Stieglitz group, were able to drastically modify their extensive modern Parisian training in order to develop American styles. Critics have banned them from the mainstream of Modern Art for their betrayal of the Modernist aesthetic. The few Modernist critics who mention Benton and Rivera emphasize the influence of synchronism and Cubism in their murals but underplay the much more pervasive inspiration of the baroque in Benton and early Renaissance in Rivera.

International Modernism

An informative study could compare early American Modernism to the styles of artists from other countries who traveled to Paris to study, such as the English Bloomsbury group. We see the same youthful verve give way to confusion and sapped energy, and a renewed interest in subject matter. Duncan Grant's childlike variations on Matisse retrogressed into traditional English landscapes. Even Roger Fry, who brought Modern Art to England in two blockbuster exhibitions of French art, in the end painted traditional landscapes.

Postwar Art

It is frequently said that Abstract Expressionism eclipsed previous American art, that earlier styles were spin-offs of European prototypes or clunky provincialisms. Then the postwar New York school finally came up with its own original world-class abstractions, and this self-proclaimed supreme effort of American artists came when European art was eclipsed by the war.

In the 1950s there was the second coming of abstraction to the promised land: New York. After the shift of cultural power, American enthusiasm reinvented all the Modernist ideas, simplifying, bastardizing, and finally commercializing them.

The media could not get enough of the new "isms": after the shock and awe of Abstract Expressionism came Pop, Op, Minimalism, Neo-expressionist, Neo-geo, Installation, and Post-Modern (to name the most prominent). For all the hype, our proliferating movements were hardly as original as their early twentieth century counterparts.

Abstract Expressionism

Abstract Expressionism was the last gasp of the non-objective art movement, which was forty years old. In my opinion, its vaunted American strengths, bigness and boldness, are weaknesses compared to the original European abstractionists. The Americans never had the earlier artists' tension between two- and three-dimensional space. Eventually, Americans gave up composition altogether. The New York school contributed unlimited self-indulgence. With a lack of historical resonance, Abstract Expressionism was reduced to the various artists' monomanias. De Kooning is criticized for being conservative, retaining vestiges of his European background, such as the shallow space and central image that hark back to Cubism. Conversely, Pollock is praised, the anarchistic chaos of his work considered a quality.

De Kooning, Pollock and Kline have in common Harold Rosenberg's concept of action painting, that the existential act is more important than the result. The artistic climax is in the process of creating. The public is to get excited vicariously, sensing the excitement in the resulting art. (I don't make this up). The other branch of Abstract Expressionism can hardly be called action painting, as there are large expanses of unvarying color surfaces.

In the Abstract Expressionist wings of various museums, the public wanders aimlessly through cavernous halls featuring gigantic canvases. There is nothing to focus the eye on.

Art experts are ceaselessly promoting oversize museums to house vast quantities of outsized modern American art. They turn abandoned factories into the world's largest art depositories, monuments to late capitalism. The art establishment claims that these acres of inflated art represent the highest expression of Western culture.

The Abstract Expressionists were promoted as the last giants of the art world. In reality they were dysfunctional hangers-on, lost souls. They had a burst of belated creativity, a lashing out in impotent alcoholic rage. Then they self-destructed. These are our heroes.

Arshile Gorky

Arshile Gorky impressed people as a childlike giant. He is often seen as a forerunner of Abstract Expressionism. While it's true that Gorky influenced some of their early work, they didn't come into their own styles until they moved past his biomorphic and surrealist borrowings.

Clyfford Still and Barnett Newman

Clyfford Still was the worst artist of the group. His huge expanses of slick, dark paint with their predictable little flat flame-shapes don't justify his self-glorification.

Barnett Newman's work is said to harbor heavy philosophical concepts. His "zips," or thin bright lines, like Still's flames, are surrounded by boring expanses of unremitting paint.

Mark Rothko

Rothko's paint surface is more inviting and his work has a pure sense of decoration, but do these pleasantnesses add up to some ultimate bliss? What I find bland induces nirvana in some viewers.

Jackson Pollock

Jackson Pollock's off-putting aggressiveness counters the empathy needed to lose oneself in the labyrinth of attenuated drippings. It's not a pleasant place, with its globs, slick enamel and occasional cigarette butts. Pollack creates an impressively intricate network. How often could (or should) a man repeat that performance?

Willem de Kooning

De Kooning's youthful style displayed clumsy, stilted figures. His apologists claimed he could draw like Ingres. It was a relief when de Kooning relaxed into his flamboyantly painterly Abstract style.

When de Kooning reintroduced the figure in his *Woman* series, there was excitement and controversy in the art world, a sad reflection on the status of figuration. The Greenbergian formalists hated to see subject matter reappear.

His return to the figure was, among other things, a return to his earlier clumsiness. Seen positively, the *Woman* series' obsessiveness is exciting, particularly because of the edgy misogyny. De Kooning never resolved the figurative elements, but rather retreated to a more reserved, elegant style.

There is an edge of disgust in de Kooning's paintings. The colors are liverish. The wet paint excessively worked, shapes barely congealing.

Patterns don't emerge, but waver around an unresolved central image. Action painting can have a high quotient of frustration and wasted energy. De Kooning tempers the compulsive angst with some European suavity. We sense the dandy. His style easily devolves into mannerism.

Post-Abstract Expressionism

Robert Rauschenberg and Jasper Johns subverted Abstract Expressionism, pushing its tendentiousness over the edge into decadence. Inflated macho was transmuted into a gay joke. Heroic flinging of paint became a campy gesture. Cosmic invocations gave way to ready-mades. While undermining the grandiloquence of the New York school, Rauschenberg and Johns nevertheless retained their prerogatives of superstar status. They played to the inflated art world, saying, in effect, "We can do it too, and so much more cleverly."

Andy Warhol

Andy Warhol's showmanship went further; it became the whole of his art. Warhol turned Harold Rosenberg's theory of action painting on its head. If action is the determining factor, then why not just admit that the actor is the art? The artist's persona, what he does, how his actions are perceived; that's the art. To Warhol the creative act is the manipulation of the media. Art is there to remind us of the artist's public image. When one thinks about Warhol, it's difficult to visualize the oeuvre but all too easy to have a concept of Warhol himself, with his reptilian face, drugs, deviation, vulgar display, vacuousness. Warhol became the paradigmatic artist, the apotheosis of Modern Art. The traditional values of art have all been superseded. Yet the apparatus of art "appreciation" is gloriously intact. The art world has grown, has become, in fact, so highly developed that it is now perfect in and of itself. The art world generates its own meanings. Their pronouncements trickle down and the rest of the world goes along.

Pop Art

The Pop artists took the neo-Dada gambits of Rauschenberg, Johns and Warhol, and vulgarized and codified them. Imagery came back as a backlash to the ambiguity of Abstract Expressionism. The return of subject matter took the form of a glorification of our materialist culture.

Minimalism

After these excesses there was a seeming reaction toward purism in the art world. The Minimalists and still more minimal Conceptualists claimed to purge art of conspicuous consumption. "Less is more" is an oxymoron that might be expected to give pause to even the most determined art lover. The essence of art could be distilled, embodied in less and less form and content, until only the conception mattered. It could exist without appearing. With Minimalism the art establishment is publicly chastised, but privately very much still there, a society of the elect.

Conceptual, Minimal, Earth and Installation, Performance, Body Art—these movements claim altruism in forgoing galleries and sales, abjuring the pleasures of consumer society. If they were sincere, we would never have heard of them. Their aesthetic extremism was precisely because they were so secure in their establishment patronage. They could sit back and wait for the cult followers, the foundations, the National Endowment for the Arts (NEA), the D.I.A., the magical serendipity of the MacArthur grant. The "less" of their art is the "more" of their supporting system.

If the public were not in thrall to the art experts, who would willingly contemplate blank canvases, rows of bricks, and pseudo-Euclidean diagrams scribbled on a museum wall?

Post-Modernists

The Post-Modernists owned up to the emptiness at the end of

reductive avant-gardism. Yet and still, they did not see fit to abandon the art world apparatus. There was still momentum in the fact that now it didn't make any difference what was fed into the system. To the Post-Modern way of thinking there is no intrinsic value, only what is assigned. These new artists decided to make self-consciously uncreative works. No more naïve obligation to create something of value. One might think that anyone could come up with something valueless, but only the most select artists can be in the right place at the right time, perfectly in sync. Only the select can conceive the art that will deconstruct what came before. And really, how different is this from the avant-garde agenda?

A side effect of deconstruction is pluralism, more democratic and thus disturbing to the experts. The idea here is to give up the whole game. Movements didn't supersede each other after all. Now we can see that they were all equally valid. There were good artists in every period. They all had something in their own contexts in this view. Surely there must be an audience capable of appreciation for any and every work of art, somewhere, sometime. Everybody deserves their own aesthetic experience. The free enterprise system will keep moving this stuff around.

Only on this lowest common denominator level are the strictures of the high art scene questioned. Fine, say the Post Modernists, if the official art world wants to maintain an ultra-refined coterie. But does that give them the right to dictate taste, to dominate the NEA, the Whitney, *Art in America* and so on?

One critic facetiously suggested that the Whitney Biennial should exhibit the artists who spent the most money advertising their art. This pluralist thinking opens a Pandora's Box of populist ideas. There could be museum shows for the most popular artists, the most prolific artists, the highest-priced artists, the slickest artists, the most popular teachers, the inventors of the last 100 isms.

Summation

Modern Art, taken as a whole, divorced itself from common experience and from the values that celebrate life. Like most religions, Modern Art sets up a mind-body dichotomy, with mind being abstraction, and body as perception and sensation. Duchamp's greatest contempt was for what he called "Retinal Art". As the avant-garde became established, hermetic concepts took the place of our common response to the world, responses that could be embodied in Realism.

Final Meditation

Modernism was a time of revision, finding it invigorating to question old notions. Received knowledge was bound to feel oppressive to the ignorant, especially if the student already wanted to be different. As we discussed, perspective and shading were anathema to Cézanne. Since Cézanne, most people were glad to dispense with those disciplines, although by now I would think that reverse perspective and flatness would have gone stale, and been perceived as more restrictive than perspective and shading had ever been.

Since 1863, the year of the Salon des Refusés, the techniques of art have been progressively abandoned. Now, with deconstruction, traditional concepts of artistic structure are really beyond comprehension.

What else can we do except poke around in the rubbish heap of styles, while quipping that whatever we find will have no viable meaning anyway?

Traditional-minded artists are perceived as being dense to think they can breathe new life into systems that, properly deconstructed, are perceived as never having been valid.

Before our sophisticated time, artists were unashamed of learning from earlier styles. When contexts shifted, the resulting tensions were often seen as adding complexity, rather than the loss of meaning implied by "slipping signifiers." The Pre-Raphaelites wanted to recapture the freshness of creativity that they perceived existed before mannerism and baroque art. Though their paintings cannot be mistaken for those of the early Italians, they did achieve an intensity that revitalized Victorian art. Artists in earlier periods hardly doubted the meaning of their work. Is it possible to forsake Modern and Post-Modern, and to try consciously to be premodern? While artists can't literally return to a previous century, we can try to reconstitute the wholeness of vision that was possible then. There is always the threat of a lifeless rehash. Perhaps a strong sense of purpose would mitigate against this. As Degas said, "An artist can't help but be of his own time." So why try not to be?

Why shouldn't art embody the will to contemplate and even celebrate life? Who doesn't enjoy light, space, the things of the world? Why shouldn't artists use the old techniques such as shading and perspective that make it possible to celebrate in art what we care for in life?

Enough of artists wanting to be different and divisive. Better to be comprehensible and inclusive.

The negative modern gospel is that artists don't use the old ways because they want to express something new. Just the opposite is true. Modern artists are afraid of being truly different. There is a sameness in their wanting only to be avant-garde. For a hundred years the unforgivable sin has been to not do the latest thing. The wrath of the whole art establishment comes down on the traditionalist, the academician, the retarditaire. To try to paint as well as artists from other centuries did is many times more original than to subscribe to the "shock of the new".

Modern Art schools have courses in conceptual art, installation art, performance art, and Post-Modernism. Admittedly, they also include a drawing class, but it is drawing in name only, not even touching on the perspective, shading, and anatomy that were studied for eight years in the academy system.

There are historical precedents for a backwards-looking movement. We mentioned the Pre-Raphaelites. The Renaissance (rebirth) resurrected classical themes despite the Catholic Church and its Byzantine iconography. The Neoclassicists extolled Roman virtue in the face of monarchy and the Rococo. Diego Rivera and the Social Realists painted radical Realist murals despite capitalism and its abstractions.

Think of Vermeer as opposed to Warhol. Vermeer gives the viewer a sense of being in the world, of being almost supernaturally present in the room depicted. The viewer is projected into a harmonious existence. Warhol gives us the opposite effect. Warhol is ubiquitous. He is master of the media; the media has become the world. The viewer is promised a vicarious fifteen minutes of fame.

Are painters so in thrall to a self-perpetuating elitist system that they can no longer conceive of socially responsible art? It is possible the public is so brainwashed that there is no interest in art concerned with traditional humanist interests. At least I have had my say and I hope you have heard me out.

To many of my readers my opinions will seem extreme and ill-considered. It has been a daunting task to articulate ideas that are opposed to almost everything written about Modern Art. As a Realist painter, I have long had my doubts about avant-garde art and have resented the one-sided critical praise. I realize that many of my perceptions will seem rashly presented and lacking in precedent. Nevertheless, to clarify my opinions and to share them with others who have had doubts about Modern Art, I determined to write them down.

Notes

Notes

Notes